Rare Is Everywhere

Deborah Katz

Miss Bird Books

Vancouver, BC

First hardcover and eBook editions published in February 2017 by Miss Bird Books

www.rareiseverywhere.com

Cataloguing data available from Library and Archives Canada

ISBN 978-0-9958261-0-6 (hardcover)
ISBN 978-0-9958261-1-3 (eBook)

First Edition

Production & Editorial: Behind the Book (www.behindthebook.ca)
Design: Michela Sorrentino, H+S Design (www.hermanidesign.com)

Proceeds from the sale of this book will be donated to the Rare Disease Foundation.

RARE DISEASE
FOUNDATION

This book has been supported by our generous sponsors:

CASCADIA
METALS

CHEO
RESEARCH INSTITUTE

help at home

J.COREA
GROUP

Printed and bound in Canada by Friesens

For Miriam, Dustin, and children everywhere
— may you always know how beautiful you are.

What Does Rare Mean?

To be rare is to be different in a special way.

Like the...

Sporty Spotless Cheetah

There isn't another in the world like me
A cheetah has spots, so what could I be?
People think I'm a lion or other fierce cat
They've never seen a cheetah quite like that!

My cheetah friends have 2,000 spots,
I don't have any – just a few tiny dots.
Unlike lions and tigers that come out at night,
With my great speed, I hunt prey in daylight.

I'm the fastest animal that roams the land,
They call me golden – I'm the color of sand.
I blend with the grass and am hard to spot
Spotless I am, but slow I am not!

Brilliant Blue Lobster

Lobsters are reddish-brown, I'm the only one that's blue
Even stranger than that, there are yellow ones too!

I never stop growing, so I can become very large,
I use my claws to eat and show others who's in charge.
I live on the ocean floor and eat all kinds of prey,
I hunt mostly at night and rest during the day.

Some people catch lobsters to cook as a treat
If you catch a blue one, set it free — they're too rare to eat!

Alert Albino Deer

My nose is pink and my eyes shine bright,

I have no spots and my fur is white.

All summer long I am easy to see

If a predator is near, I have to flee.

I wake up early and nap in the day

Then come out at night, to eat and to play.

I grow new antlers in spring each year

Then shed them again as winter draws near.

When winter comes, I blend with the snow

I'm protected from hunting wherever I go.

Beloved Black Penguin

Instead of black wings and a bright white chest
I have black feathers that I wear like a vest.
I am easy to see next to all the others
My baby can find me among all the mothers.

My black feathers warm me in the freezing cold air,
It's like wearing a pair of long underwear!
I swim like a rocket and catch fish to eat
I dive deep for squid – a big tasty treat.

I lay one egg and keep it still, safe, and warm
In daytime and nighttime – through every ice storm.
When my chick hatches, I teach it to glide
Into the sea on a great waterslide!

Big Brown Panda

My friends are black and white, but I'm dark and light brown,

There are only a few of us that have ever been found.

It may be the water or the food that I eat

That makes me the color of chocolate and wheat.

I mostly sleep and eat bamboo in the day,

My thumbs help me hold it just the right way.

I live in the mountains, where few people go

I spend lots of time resting and move pretty slow.

I'm known far and wide for my soft furry fleece

And am loved by all people as a symbol of peace.

Watchful White Alligator

I have shiny white scales and bright blue eyes,

When people see me, they gasp in surprise.

I need to be in shade, where I can swim and run,

My skin has no color, it burns in the sun.

I am as large as other gators, and I live just as long,

My diet is the same as theirs, and my jaw is just as strong.

What do I eat? I'll tell you right now

I like to eat birds, and I'll tell you how.

I put twigs on my head and leaves by the bunch

When they land on me, I eat them for lunch!

Bold Black Jaguar

My fur is black while on others it's gold

I may look different, but I'm just as bold!

When you look closely, you can see my spots

They blend with my fur and look like pale dots.

I climb trees in the jungle to wait for my prey,

Then pounce down quickly so they can't get away.

Like my cousin the tiger, I am a good swimmer

And when I am wet, my black fur shimmers.

There are 600 of us in the world today

We don't have much land, or places to play.

We are magical and powerful and tricky to see,

In the heart of the jungle — that's where we run free.

Spectacular Spirit Bear

The Great Bear Rainforest is my home

Way up north, I ramble and roam.

I am really a black bear, though my fur is white,

In the middle of the forest, I am quite a sight!

My parents can be white, but they can also be black

We are the same in most ways, except for one fact.

I'm better at catching fish – they don't see me coming by

Because of my white fur, I blend into the sky.

Legend says I was made white a long time ago

To remind us of the Ice Age, when the world was under snow.

When winter comes, I will sleep in my den

I'll be catching salmon right until then!

Pretty Pink Grasshopper

Unlike other hoppers I'm pink, not green

I can jump very high, but I'm easily seen.

I don't blend with the leaves or with the grass

There's no place to hide — it's lucky I'm fast.

I have very large eyes on the sides of my face,

I use antennae to smell, and my mouth to taste.

When I want to talk I rub my legs against my wings

You can hear me in the bushes — my whole body sings!

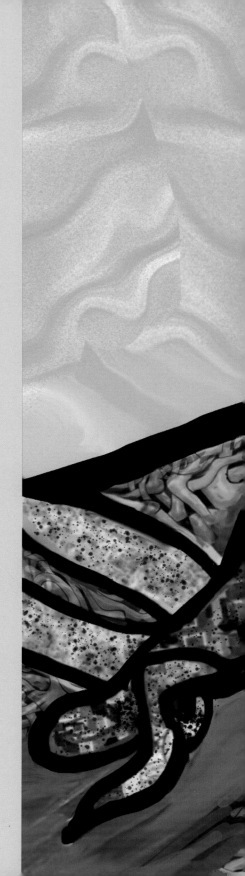

Wise White Tiger

My fur is white and my eyes are light blue

I have excellent vision, and great hearing too.

No matter the color, all tigers have stripes

Every pattern is different — no two are alike.

I'm rare among cats in that I love to get wet

You can often find me swimming, on that I would bet.

I run fast and run hard, nothing gets in my way,

When I'm not hunting, I'm sleeping — 18 hours a day!

Except when I have cubs, I mostly live alone

You can find me in the jungle, the place I call home.

I'm a symbol of strength and a symbol of power

When other animals see me, they run and they cower!

So if you ever feel different,
like a white spirit bear,

You don't have to worry,
because...

Rare is EVERYWHERE!

About the Animals

The animals in this book are rare because of changes in their genes. Genes are too small to see without a special microscope, but every animal has them, including people. Genes carry information that makes us who we are, including what we look like. Genes make people and animals different from each other in surprising and amazing ways!

Spotless Cheetah

Not much is known about what makes a cheetah spotless. There is only one known spotless cheetah in the world today. It was "spotted" a few years ago in Kenya, Africa. Before that, the last time a spotless cheetah was seen was 100 years ago!

Blue Lobster

Blue lobsters have bright blue-colored shells instead of the reddish-brown ones that lobsters usually have. Catching a blue lobster is thought to bring good luck to the fisherman. Like other lobsters, blue lobsters can live for 70 years or longer. Only one in every 2 million lobsters is blue!

Albino Deer

Albino deer do not have any coloring in their fur or skin. They have white fur, pink noses, and light eyes. Albino deer are just like other deer, except that they may not see as well. Many people believe white deer are special and bring good luck. One in every 20,000 deer is albino.

Black Penguin

The all-black penguin is a king penguin, the second largest penguin in the world (the emperor is the largest). It has melanism — a change in its genes that makes it have black feathers on its chest where usually they would be white. One in 250,000 penguins has some black feathers on its chest, but only one penguin in the world has black feathers all over its body.

Brown Panda

Brown pandas have dark and light brown fur instead of black and white fur. They live in the Qinling Mountains of China. Only a handful of brown pandas have been spotted in the last 30 years, and there is only one brown panda in the world today.

White Alligator

The white alligator is not a true albino alligator because it has some coloring in its body and eyes. White alligators are rare in the wild. Out of 5 million American alligators, only 12 are white!

Black Jaguar

Black jaguars, sometimes called black panthers, also have melanism — a change in their genes that makes them have black spotted fur, whereas other jaguars are tan or golden with black spots. They live in South America, where one in 17 jaguars is a black jaguar.

Spirit Bear

Spirit bears (also called Kermode bears) are black bears that have a gene that makes their fur white. In order for a cub to be born white, both of its parents must also have this gene. Spirit bears live only in the coastal rainforests of British Columbia, Canada. They are quite rare, but on one small island in this area, as many as one-third of the bears are white.

Pink Grasshopper

Pink grasshoppers have brightly colored pink bodies instead of green bodies like other grasshoppers. It is not known exactly how often grasshoppers are born pink, but it is thought to be extremely rare.

White Tiger

White tigers are not albinos — they are actually Bengal tigers with white fur and blue eyes. White tigers are rare in the wild, but they can sometimes be found in zoos. Only one in 10,000 Bengal tigers is white.

Chimera Butterfly

The chimera butterfly, as pictured with the girl in the book, has a different pattern on one half of its body compared to the other half. It can even be half female and half male! The girl in the book has different colored eyes, which is called heterochromia.

Joke Corner

What kind of floor does an alligator like to sleep on?

One with rep-tiles!

On which side does a white tiger have the most stripes?

The outside!

What is the black jaguar's favorite color?

Purr-ple!

How does the spirit bear catch salmon without a fishing rod?

With its bear hands!

What do you call a grasshopper that likes to clean the floor?

A grassmopper!

What is the black penguin's favorite thing to eat for dinner?

An ice-berger!

What kind of deer loves to get wet?

A rain-deer!

Why is it a bad idea to play cards with the fastest animals in the world?

Because they're all cheetahs!

Why was the lobster blue?

He ate a sad fish!

What do brown pandas like to eat for breakfast?

Panda-cakes!